# CEMETERY WALKS

## AND OTHER WRITINGS BY

# DAVE BRESLIN

Order this book online at www.trafford.com/08-1407
or email orders@trafford.com

Most Trafford titles are also available at major online book retailers.

Note for Librarians: A cataloguing record for this book is available from Library and Archives Canada at www.collectionscanada.ca/amicus/index-e.html

Printed in Victoria, BC, Canada.

Design and writings By Dave Breslin.
Cover photo taken by Charles F. Tilton (Posthumously).
Also Available by Dave Breslin: This Sober Life (2002).
For more information visit: www.DaveBreslin.com

ISBN: 978-1-4251-8970-9

*We at Trafford believe that it is the responsibility of us all, as both individuals and corporations, to make choices that are environmentally and socially sound. You, in turn, are supporting this responsible conduct each time you purchase a Trafford book, or make use of our publishing services. To find out how you are helping, please visit www.trafford.com/responsiblepublishing.html*

*Our mission is to efficiently provide the world's finest, most comprehensive book publishing service, enabling every author to experience success. To find out how to publish your book, your way, and have it available worldwide, visit us online at www.trafford.com/10510*

www.trafford.com

North America & international
toll-free: 1 888 232 4444 (USA & Canada)
phone: 250 383 6864 ♦ fax: 250 383 6804
email: info@trafford.com

The United Kingdom & Europe
phone: +44 (0)1865 487 395 ♦ local rate: 0845 230 9601
facsimile: +44 (0)1865 481 507 ♦ email: info.uk@trafford.com

10 9 8 7 6 5 4 3 2

# FOR ME

# CEMETERY WALKS

## I. WINTER

# II. SPRING

# III. SUMMER

# IV. AUTUMN

# I. WINTER

*------------ Pitch black, silent and twenty-eight degrees,*
*I thought it similar to what death must be like. -----------*

**Who Would I Be**

Outside, I walk nervous and unsettled through a parking lot toward a school wondering who I'd be had I not known so well the feelings of such pain and self-doubt, the taste of an ice-cold beer on a summer night, the euphoria, the invincibility, the confidence of a subtle buzz, the smiles and carefree laughs brought on by the drunken foolishness of young men before we knew the extent of our foolishness, the feeling of acceptance by myself and others that I have found my role and should go with it because it seems to fit, the taste of bloodied gums from quick jabs to the face invited by my inability to keep quiet due to certain mind state, the scent of puke running through my nose while sleeping to wake soaked in sweat and guilt with mind crushing headache and dehydrated fevered skin, the warm taste of the last sip from a left over beer swallowed only to forget the night before, the encounters with hypocritical, arrogant, crooked cops using unnecessary force to handcuff a drunk, one hundred and thirty pound, nineteen year old, to satisfy their need for inflation of self worth that never really satisfies, the shameful looks of disgusted witnesses of my sickness, the memories of days upon days spent with close friends I'd soon lose to death, the realization of myself as someone society has told me is hopeless and worthless.

I step inside to where I'm looked up to and admired for knowing the things I wish I didn't and I begin to wonder who I would be without all the nights spent alone in bed pleading to a God I didn't believe in to, "At least let me sleep if you won't let me die." Who would I be without the embarrassment left from admittance of weakness to those I've displayed and insisted only strength in front of, the days where tears ran dry but it mattered nothing because I was still crying, the depression endlessly begging for freedom that it explains is found only in suicide and stays insistent through months of dosage upon higher dosage of medication that not only makes you sick but doesn't help the depression, the waking from a suicide attempt, the waking from a suicide attempt to realize I was the only one who knows it was attempted at all, the idea that the taste of tears on your lips is worse than the feeling of pushing a blade against your wrist wondering how well it can cut as you think to yourself, "This would stop the tears." Who would I be without the memories and images of scenario upon scenario of how and when I'd do it or without knowing the sight and the sound and the shake of the ground as a bright lighted train stares at you, moves closer and then from 30 yards away you begin to second guess whether it would work or not and then you take that small step away and it passes?

Who would I be without knowing the nervousness felt while a jury deliberates your guilt, the countless hours of solitude, the guilt you feel for becoming so dependent upon others just to free yourself of your dependencies, the pessimistic attitude that has evolved out of my seemingly endless string of bad luck, the endless self doubt and lack of self esteem that has brought anxiety whenever expected to carry on a conversation sober, the lack of trust that seems to have grown from the things I still won't write or talk about, the poetry, the self evaluation, all the realizations and the acceptance of myself?

I meet the students and I have to wonder who I'd be without knowing the feeling of my best friends ice cold forehead against my lips as I kissed him while he was lying in his coffin, the weight of the coffin, the color, the feel, the nylon liner, the texture of the wood on the coffin, the sight of the coffin as it left in the hearse, the shock six months later as I heard the news that the friend who comforted me as I sat at the coffin shot himself and now lies in his own coffin, another coffin and another and another. Who would I be without knowing the helplessness you feel as you try to wake another friend as he twitches in and out of a coma and the stare of his eyes catch yours every time they rapidly open and close, the stare that can only be explained as blank and empty, the intuition that my friends are not done dying, the lonely cemetery walks taken to evoke the idea that I still have friends, the calls from friends who are now in the same place I once was and are about to know all of what I know, the fact that I know no matter what I say, write or do or how much I want it, nothings going to change unless they really want it to?

I read aloud the thoughts of my past while wondering who I would be without the confusion felt for being admired for survival by strangers, friends and those who thought nothing of me but now look up to me for knowing the things I look down on, things I wish I never knew.

I wonder what they would say if I told them that what I really want them all to know is that no one should know all this, no one should admire me for this and no one should look up to me for this.

Look down on me. You don't want to know what I know, stop trying to learn for yourself. Look up to yourself for not needing to know. Success is not succeeding through failure; success is not failing. That is admirable, that is what I look up to and that is who I would be without knowing all of this. I'd be successful, I'd be admirable and I would be someone to look up to.
I'd be you.

# Eyes

I look into my eyes.
I look into a broken mirror.
I have dropped my disguise.
I am beginning
to see things clearer.

I look into my eyes.
I look at a reflective teardrop.
I've got scars on my mind,
thoughts that bleed
and just will not stop.

Come look into my eyes,
look at them past the flesh and tissue.
Come with me as I walk you through
the dark alleys
that are my mind.

Come look into my eyes.
See the scenes that will not leave me,
feel the pain I feel inside me,
think the thoughts
you hear in my mind.

Close your eyes now.
Close your eyes,
look at your mind.
Are you about to become me
or will you set your sights
not to die?

**Rainy Day**

Rain reminds me of everything that I carry below the surface.
I'm constantly covering up just to stay dry.
Days like this leave my eyes feeling stagnant in my own head.
Cold, heavy and thoughtless I wait to fade into the next day as if
today is already spent.
I question whether it is the day itself that leaves me depressed, the
idea that days like this make me depressed or if it is that I
subconsciously see rainy days mixed in with dry days as a fitting
metaphor for life and I am just simply falling into my preconceived
role for the day.

## Lawrence Street

There is a graveyard and behind it runs a dirt road along a river,
the water foams from pollution and trash floats throughout it.
Across the river sits an old abandoned shack, it's painted
farmhouse red but it's chipped and beat.
Along the banks of the river, trash, glass, used rubbers and needles
lie scattered.
In over grown brush you can find remnants from past squatters
and empty bottles of booze.
One day while I stood pissing from the bank into the river I looked
around and thought, "This place is somehow beautiful."

**Pinwheel**

A breeze blows a pinwheel stuck in the ground. I'll call anything a
sign these days.

It's a bit odd, all this living that I do day by day, the worries, the
goals, the things I achieve, I realize they're all so meaningless
whenever I sit here.

It's always quiet here. The silence matches the images inside my
head. There's regret in the air. There is always regret here.
The things I forget, the things I never said, the things I try to forget
I never said.

Sometimes, even just for a second it feels like you might come
back. Like the images would just fill back up with sound and the
air would clear of regret,
then it passes and I have to deal with it all over again.

I used to cry, I wish I still could, I don't know why I don't, I want
to cry, it would hurt less.
Crying without tears is just painful and empty,
it's a lot like when you see something that you have to turn away
from in disgust. How do you turn away from your mind or the
images and memories that bounce around in it?

I imagine it sometimes, your death.
What you must've been thinking just before.
Did it hurt?
I hope it didn't hurt.
We used to get so drunk sometimes, so drunk we were numb.
I hope you were numb.
I try to convince myself you were.

Sometimes it works.
Sometimes I ask the pinwheel in the ground.

Yeah, I talk to the pinwheel now.

Sometimes it moves at the perfect time, almost as if it's answering
me for you and for that second, I have hope.

People think I'm strong now. I know I'm not.
I'm just numb. Your death and my life have numbed me.

Everybody thought I'd drink when you died. They were worried
about telling me or leaving me alone. I knew I wouldn't, it was the
first time I felt anything all year.

I wanted to feel it.

It was the worst thing I've ever felt. It's weird wanting to feel a
pain but at the same time wishing it wasn't there at all. It's a little
like this grave.

Your parents got a nice stone, they plant flowers to make it look
nice, I put this bench here to sit and write, we try to make it like
you would want it, you know, perfect. But really, you wouldn't
want this grave. You wouldn't want a grave at all, you wouldn't
want flowers or benches or this fucking pinwheel.

You'd want to be alive.

But you're not, and all we have is this grave, these flowers, this
bench, this pinwheel, our memories and our pain. It's not enough
so I write these poems searching for enough,
It's never enough.

## Sell Yourself

Are you actively functioning
or in the act of expiring?
This is the difference between
living and dying.
Were you born to die or
were you given life?
To me it seems simple
but I've seen both sides.
Don't open your eyes,
open your mind,
listen closely to
your voice inside.
Behind all the ego
and social role,
lies all that you say to
yourself when  alone.
That is you, whether you
you like it or not
and unless you share your
own inner thoughts;
you will truly expire
before you are bought.

## Wake Up

Early Sunday morning, just before the sun comes,
someone's standing high above us.
No one seems to notice, it's too well that he knows this
so he throws himself right down on us.

All across the same town there's someone hiding something
they don't want the world to notice.
Rapists, thieves and murderers and though you may not think so
it is affecting every single one of us.

The church bells ring and millions of Americans
smile out their windows at the same sun,
some over the weather, almost none over each other
and most over their own reflection.

With one rotation of the earth a new day has been born,
the news displays to us the afterbirth.
No one's ever shocked, it never seems to stop
and we wonder why we're all so fucking lost.

## Change

I'm starting to think there's no use.
I'm starting to think nothing's worth it.
I'm starting to think nothing's ever going to change.
I'm starting to think just like everybody else.

How much does it take for all of us to open our eyes and see that things aren't just going to fix themselves? How many eyes have to be rolled, how many people have to laugh and say, "Here we go again, another tree hugging, free loving, happy horse shit mutherfucker is talking about love and fixing the earth and all of its problems." How many people have to say this before we realize that we only think this way because of the egos we've all been taught to fake?

And look how far that has gotten us.

These days everything is about what everybody else is doing wrong. The only truth in that is that everybody is doing wrong. If everybody pointed a finger at someone we'd all have a finger pointed at us, in a room of two people or in a world of six billion and that's just it, we are all to blame.

We are where we are and we're all so fucked up and lost because no one has the balls to stand up and be themselves or speak up and say the truth. The truth is that this whole fucking world has gone to shit and it's not getting better and as much as we tell ourselves it isn't our fault or however many people we point at for fucking it all up it isn't making it better. The truth is that it's my fault, it's your fault, it's our teachers, our mothers, our fathers and everybody who has ever and is now walking this earth. It is every one of us and the problem is that we just point fingers and say things like, "It's him because he looks like that." or, "It's her because she acts like that." or, "It was me but now I don't do that." Well that hasn't worked, it doesn't work and as much as you might feel like it's working for you, it's not. Just ask the Asians or the Latinos or the blacks or the Jews, or the Indians or the white man or the witches or Satan. It's fake and it's making you more and more at fault because you won't even acknowledge it. That's what happens, we see something for long enough not getting better and we just label it with sayings like, "If you can't beat them, join them." And then, we become them and things don't get better, they multiply and then we forget that we even want them better and we become lost.

So instead of staying lost, find yourself and when someone starts complaining about who's fault it is, tell them that it's all of our faults and that unless we all realize that this, "every man for himself" egotistical attitude isn't working and that we all have to take the blame as a whole and fix it as a whole or else it's just going to continue to become a bigger and bigger hole until we all fall in.

## Cemetery Walks

There's something about the sound of your own footsteps in a cemetery, it's almost as if you're defining and comparing the difference between life and death with each steps beat.

Some days I walk heavily, stomping my feet, snapping my fingers and listening to the echo through the silent air.

Other days I walk without noticing sound at all.

But from time to time, I slow myself to a dragging stop, hold my breath, close my eyes and listen real close.

## December Sixth

The winter always leaves me with such memories.
The winter always leaves me admiring those with memories
      of sugar plums and smiles.
Last winter, on this day, someone I knew blew out the back of his
head because he couldn't find a ride to the methadone clinic.
It's three weeks until Christmas.

I've heard people comment on how beautiful snow is.
I used to get drunk whenever there was a snowstorm.
It almost always felt like a holiday or an excuse to tie one on.
It still does.
It's not beautiful.

It gets dark early in the winter,
so does my mood,
in the summer it's not until late
but it's all day in the winter.

The cold makes you feel so tight, no way around it just tight.
Extra layers make you feel hidden, heavy and stiff,
like a body in a casket.

What the hell is a sugar plum anyway?

## Solitude

I've got a negative intuition
with positive results,
I truly wish it differently
but I've yet to see anything else.
I can't find it in my television,
newspaper is no help,
both are justification that this
world has gone to hell.
I avoid answering my telephone,
I'm afraid of what I'll hear,
"Another friend has lost the fight."
or, "Can you bail me out of jail?"
I've tried to go out and socialize
with old friends and so-called peers,
it does nothing for me and it's scary to see
their futures so blatantly clear.
This life I lead now is somewhat bitter
but it's also slightly sweet.
Solitude gets lonely but it is
my safest company.

**Ten Bucks**

*I have ten bucks ----- you can have it but promise me it's not for*
*    drugs.*
*It's not, I promise.*
*Food and cigarettes but no drugs.*
*I promise ----- Thanks Dave.*

I knew it would go to drugs but I just had to say it first.  I always
stayed my ground with him.  He knew I didn't like what he was
doing but he also knew that I wouldn't talk down to him about it.
One night I even said it,

*There's only two ways out of this shit.*
*I know*
*You're gonna die man, you're killing yourself.*

I've had this intuition before about friends.  It comes true.  It
doesn't make me happy.  I'd much rather be wrong in everything
than always right in these instances.
Now I question whether there was anything I could've done.

**January 22<sup>nd</sup> 2005**

Today, it was five years ago that I awoke shattered as a person and torn between a decision to carry on inviting chaos into my life, end my life or to reevaluate myself and learn how to live without excuses. In retrospect, the right decision seems so obvious but the weakness I was so used to carrying left me at a loss when it came to acting on my own. While the past five years has changed me in so many ways, there is still one thought that remains a ringing bell, a thought I heard so early on in my struggle toward independence. Now, at a point in which my sobriety has surpassed the amount of time I spent dependant, I can't help but reflect on how much control I have on how relevant either one should be, has been or will be in my life.

I remember clearly how unsatisfying the idea of AA hit me when I realized the majority of the people I sat with in most meetings had been there five, ten and some twenty years, week after week, some even daily, still living with their past as so much a part of their present. It was just this thought that turned me off to this traditional route and with the idea that I wouldn't become this way and that what I wanted to leave in the past would someday be just that, I fought through recovery on my own towards what I'm sure many would have predicted was to be a path of failure but with time now as the only thing that could and has been the true teller, I do wrestle with the question of how successful I have been.

In sobriety I am completely successful and I now know that I have gained the tools needed to remain that way and I plan to. As far as not allowing my past to remain so relevant in my present, I'm just not sure how well I've done or how much I should try to. As a drunk, to many I was known for just that and now that I'm sober, I'm known for just that by more than as many. Both are due to my own actions but neither was ever expected.

I have learned that it is part of my personal nature to, though I'm not proud of it, dwell on things and allow them to occupy my thoughts more than I'd like. I accept this because it is also part of my nature and interesting to me to continually learn and dissect things about myself (the current reflection not excluded). I am also aware that without my endless sifting and collecting of thoughts throughout the past five years, I would have lacked the strength and understanding to make it through. However, I don't enjoy my intentions contradicting themselves so now I'm left wondering whether it is in this aspect that I have failed to overcome my past or if my intentions were just not feasible.

As an alcoholic it is said that once an alcoholic, always an alcoholic and that whenever this theory is tested, dismissed or overlooked one is bound for disaster. Therefore, in order to beat the odds one must always remind themselves of this fact and to what exactly that disaster entails. With this being true, I can't help but realize I may have been partly off in setting realistic goals but I don't think this should be an excuse to compromise too far. I know that even in knowing all of this that I would like, now that my sobriety has surpassed my time of disaster, not to be known, categorized, or even focused on for who I once was but rather for who I have and will continue to become.

Now, five years sober, and with this thought to keep in mind and live by, I am willing to compromise with myself by stating that I accept the fact that I will always be an alcoholic but I am also declaring that an alcoholic will never again be who I am.

**Winter Stones**

Just before the spring comes when the ice and snow begin to melt, puddles wrap around the gravestones.

If you lay down in front of them so that the water is at eye level, it appears as though the stone has floated out to sea.

I've heard people say that the sea is pretty.

I'm working hard at this, "Glass is half full" thing.

## February Ninth

Tonight I took the cemetery route on my nightly run.
Pitch black, silent and twenty-eight degrees,
I thought it similar to what death must be like.

As I listened to my feet slap the pavement and my breathing
increase, I spoke to no one in particular,
"I'm not breathing this way to mock you, I swear."

Five years ago to the day my best friend died. It wasn't his
cemetery but they're all the same.

I don't believe in, as strongly as I wish for, an afterlife for the
people I've lost. I can't help that it just doesn't seem very likely to
me but it is one thing that I hope I'm wrong about and it doesn't
stop me from talking out loud to him or from picturing him looking
down on me as I ran tonight.

I'm always thinking I'm supposed to do something for him on
nights like this but I can never really think of anything good
enough and then I'm forced to realize the sad truth about what
death really does to us. It leaves us, running around with nothing
left to do but remember, hope and imagine.

# II. Spring

------------ *It's dry, and as you walk down the street carrying your umbrella, you think to yourself, "Now I have to carry this thing everywhere."* ------------

## Mourning a Friend

I heard a friend was dead last week.
Sadly, I wasn't very much surprised.
I had worried and warned him earlier this year about it.

I mourned him in my own desolate way:
Searched online for obituaries, called Las Vegas' coroners office
and dug long and hard into my memory to find his mothers maiden
name.

I came up empty.

This week I heard he was still alive.
He's doing fine and there was no overdose.
Apparently, his ex is still angry with him.
I was glad to hear he's alive but I'm still mourning him,
I can't help it.

**Caged Demons**

Two invisible cords run to my mind.

One comes from my literal and one from my metaphorically caged
   demon.

I placed them in the cages; they ran the cords.

With time, I walk further from each and the cords stretch thinner
with each step. Through the cords, I constantly hear their whispers.
From time to time, I hear them scream.  This all seems to feed and
produce thoughts and emotions that leave me stuck dwelling in one
place which indirectly restates each demons relevance.

Then I think,

This constant dissonance inside my head, the tug of war with the
cords, the anger and regret aimed at their existences, momentary
immobility and any of the yet unknown or repressed residuals that
may someday come, are prices well worth paying just to know that
their screams are lullabies, when compared to the cages I have
built for them.

## Profit

I lay down into the bed I've made,
warm and safe I'll sleep today
but I'll wake to worry anyway, I can't help it.

I've never learned or found a way
to be proud of the filth I've washed away;
I always dwell on the stains I've gained while washing.

I've walked miles through dark and stormy days,
faced every fight along the way,
turning back for only that closer look at dead enemies.

I've never reveled in victory, I've always looked to find a way
to leave my pain at their graves,
but that has only helped them to better haunt me.

Maybe all of this will change some day and I'll smile without
wondering the price I'll pay,
but for now I'll keep this close eye on my pocket.

And if I never see the day
that I use up all that I have saved,
I hope someone takes this stock and turns a profit.

## Umbrella

All at once it comes down,
soaks you and leaves you dripping,
regretting stepping outside at all.

Back inside, you dry off, and you
find a way to find your way
back outside.

This time you expect the rain.

It's dry, and as you walk down the street
carrying your umbrella, you think to yourself,
"Now I have to carry this thing everywhere."

**War On T.V**

I watched the entire war on T.V.
Never saw one drop of blood.

They show us plenty of doing on T.V.
Never show us what it does.

I think it's time to turn off the T.V.
Allow our instinct to be our judge.

All of these, "eye for an eye" philosophies
have left us blind enough.

**Life Is A Roller Coaster**

Lying with my hands folded across my stomach reminds me of death. I am sure there was a time when it wouldn't remind me of anything at all.

I wonder when it is that we lose that feeling of being invincible. It used to be that second thoughts would never come. Now as I sit strapped in, before the start of a carnival ride, I find myself examining the bolts that hold things together. I analyze how easily these things are built and even more how it could just as easily snap, which then sends me off to build a relationship with it and something much larger; life.

We build these lives for ourselves, whether it's instinctually or it's like with the ride, either way we put them together with plenty of thought and research in between and the finished product ends up fairly simple and it all seems to work out just fine. Until one day, maybe it's our bolts that have loosened or rusted or something too large has found itself depending on our strength to hold it up and just like that everything we have put together is no more and we don't even get to keep that memory of lying down with our hands folded across our stomach because by then, we can't see.

I don't know which it is; whether I started to notice how breakable things are or that I stopped remembering to forget about things like this but what bothers me most is that I'm not sure which way it is that I should try to forget.

## Church And State

Hypocrites in politics
and in silly religious outfits.
I refuse to follow in the footsteps
of some indecisive antiquist.
We pick and choose which rules to follow
and then thank a God or Goddess.
We state our views and pay out dues
to hear lies from crooked puppets.
If we are the ones choosing what's true,
doesn't that take away need for a leader?
This is what we all have to see
before we can honestly say we have freedom.

**Save Me**

Save the children, save the whales,
save the earth and save the jails,
save the church and save the trees,
it's no wonder so many want to save me.

Everyone wants to save something else.
No one notices they should be saving themselves.
The only thing that we control in this life
is how we live and how we survive.

Everything else will come and go,
that's the way it has been since long ago.
If we all spent a little more time in the mirror
all of this would become much clearer.

Recognize: Helping yourselves
is the only way to help everything else.

## Internal War

Should I hold my hate and pain inside and let it
work to destroy me?
Should I let it out, try to make it worth something,
while still it works to destroy me?
Forgiveness doesn't work for me,
forgetting never has,
redemption doesn't satisfy
or help dim out the past.
Reliving what I wish was dead
will leave me weak again.
I've killed it once, mourned it twice
and now it's back again.
I know the answer is obvious,
I know what needs to be done.
It's just hard to fight battles that don't end
even when they're won.

**Questions Answer Questions**

It's underneath scar and scab
and in between thought and speech.
Is everything that is true, left unseen?

It's seen but it's not questioned
and it's thought but it's not spoken.
Is everything that we see, left unwanted?

It's true in you and me
and it's seen by you and me.
Is everything that I question, unneeded?

**Epiphany**

Holding in the air around me,
lost between a set of breaths.
A moment flashes a half lit memory
of days I sought and welcomed death.

Falling to the thoughts among me,
a conscious state I have left,
I begin to feel as if I'm drowning
in the pain that I bereft.

Breathing out of only instinct,
I realize this is how I've been set.
I drop a tear and now I'm weeping,
less the feeling of regret.

**I've got so much on my mind**

I've got so much on my mind but I don't know where to start.
I've got so much on my mind but nothing to say or write.
I've got so much on my mind but I'm putting it all off.
I've got so much on my mind but I don't want to talk about it.
I've got so much on my mind and it's not getting any better.
I've got so much on my mind but I'm dealing with the less
    important.
I've got so much on my mind but I am good at hiding it.
I've got so much on my mind but I am just like my society.

**I Don't Even Trust The Gravestones**

Are only the good people buried?

It's always angels, crosses or smiling faces etched or carved into the face of these stones and they're always surrounded by flowers or thoughtful gifts. Some have eternal flames lit next to them as if to say that the deceased will burn in our hearts forever.

I never see Satan cast in stone atop a grave, there's never shameful messages left for everyone to see and the description is always positive. They read,

                 "Beloved"

I've never even once seen,

                 "Hated"

I'm constantly reading,

                 "You will be missed"

and never,

                 "Good Riddance"

So why is it that so many people I encounter day by day never seem to be able to live up to their own future gravestone? Will they never die? Will they not be buried? Are these people new to the world or do we lie in death just as we do in life?

## Podium

This is my podium, this is my stage,
this is my chance to speak.
I could waste it on everything you've heard before
or I could tell you the truth and be me.

This is your podium, this is your stage,
this is your chance to speak.
You can waste it dying like everyone else
or you can live for yourself and be free.

**Mood Lighting**

I leave the lights out each morning while I get ready in the bathroom because I don't like seeing myself in the mirror against full wattage.

I keep telling myself I need to put a dimmer on that switch.

In rooms without mirrors I am always looking to make sure that all possible lights are on because for some reason my mood responds negatively to half-assed lighting.

It does the same with rainy days and whenever the sun doesn't shine.

I'm not sure exactly when it was that I began noticing that I don't look as good as I'd like in certain lighting but I'm just now realizing that because of it,

The way I look never reflects the way I feel.

# III. Summer

*------------ It came to me one day as I ran, dehydrating under a hot, blistering sun, fifteen miles past exhaustion, simply to find out if I could do it. ------------*

## Last Night Leaving The Supermarket

He asked,
*Sir, sir, do you have fifty cents?*
Half shaven and dirty he looked me right in the eyes.  He couldn't
even recognize me.
Have I changed that much or is he that far gone?
I recognized him right away and I reached into my pocket,
he excited,
*"I'm just trying to get some gas for my car, no one will help me out
they think I want it for drugs, I'm just stranded out here and need
to get home."*
I couldn't find any change so I opened my wallet, I still couldn't
believe he didn't recognize me, I'm not sure If I wanted him to, it
may have been worse.
He looked at my wallet,
*"Sorry to bother you man, I just need to get back to Manchester"*
I knew it was for drugs, I pulled out a five dollar bill,
*"You sure?"*
*"Yeah man, don't worry about it."*

He used to be tough, I remember he'd fight almost anyone, I never
saw him lose.
Not anymore, he looked helpless, hopeless, he's getting his ass
kicked and he can't even see it.

I handed him the five and again, he looked me right in the eyes.
*"Thank you sir, thanks"*
He called me sir, I've known him since we were in sixth grade
together, smoking pot behind the arcade, and I think he's even a
year older than I am.
I thought,
"Why are you calling me sir?"

He took the five, thanked me again and turned away to walk back towards the store.

About a minute or so later, as I was putting the groceries in my truck, from a distance I heard,

*"Excuse me maam?"*

I looked up and I saw a woman opening her purse as he stood there looking up at her with his hand out. Still shocked, I thought back to all of the parties we were at together, all the laughs, all the euphoria, the glorification of the stupid things we'd do and brag about to each other,

*"I'll drink this whole case."*

*"You won't take another shot of that, you pussy."*

I guess it was fun then, when we didn't know any better, maybe he still doesn't, he didn't look like he was having fun though, maybe then he would have recognized me; if it was still fun or if I too, still didn't know any better.

I sat there in the car for a while and thought about getting back out and telling him who I was. I watched him as he approached each person who left the supermarket, some dug for change, others ignored him totally and avoiding eye contact they'd walk past and he'd just turn to the next,

*"Excuse me sir?"*

*"Excuse me ma'am?"*

I thought about it again,

"Have I changed that much or is he that far gone?"

For a few more minutes I watched, comparing the struggle I've seen to the one I'm seeing, compassionately relating and thinking over and over again,

"Have I changed that much or is he that far gone?"

I looked into the rear view mirror to take a look at myself and I saw all of the groceries piled up on the back seat behind me and thought,
"The ice cream's going to melt, I better go."

## Miles

All my life I've been told that covering a certain amount of ground will ensure you a certain amount in return. Many people pride themselves on this same notion, "With age comes wisdom." they'll say as they lazily watch the hands of time move them over the next mile of their life. I can agree with the idea that certain experiences can certainly leave us with inherent wisdom but I don't accept that simply sitting back as miles of life pass you by earns the same entitlement.

> Miles stretched out behind me,
> miles unseen ahead.
> Miles aren't what make me,
> it's the footprints I place in them.

I've repeated this stanza to myself on many occasions. It came to me one day as I ran, dehydrating under a hot, blistering sun, fifteen miles past exhaustion, simply to find out if I could do it. It has somewhat become my mantra whenever I catch myself allowing miles to pass me by as I sit back watching, wasting the opportunity to place some reason into them. I'll also repeat it to myself whenever I find I'm ready to give up on something or afraid to attempt it at all.

I suppose my point is that sometimes we set out to do a certain thing and we only expect something equivalent in return, but then we end up gaining something completely unexpected, like the mantra, and all that it has helped me through that may not have been, had I not taken that run. I think the same can be said for all the things that we don't attempt, thinking that because we're waiting for wisdom, that is all that we will gain.

**Truth**

There are men caged in prison who hold more freedom than most can imagine.

In places where people have seen war everyday, some know nothing but to live peacefully.

It seems unheard of but it's a matter of truth;

Your world is created by the allowance of you

## Guilt

I found a feeling not missed,
this time it was different though,

>I wasn't surprised by its return.

I found it where I didn't expect to but

>I wasn't surprised, I was saddened.

Saddened because I have known to look there but hadn't on
purpose and even more so because I left it there and may never be
able to forget it.

>But for now, I had to.

**I Was Stuck On What To Say**

The way that I was spoken to confused me, I knew how to answer
but I didn't want to.

It's sad because I know the difference between what was said and
what was thought, I also know they don't think so.

I know they thought that I felt hurt as a result. I know they said
they didn't care.

I know what hurt me.

I know it wasn't what they said and that it was what they knew
and that I knew
and that for that they would hurt.

## Morning's Here

Daily, I find myself searching for and grasping onto any hope that
my next day will be better.

Glucosomine, chrondriton, msm, a multi vitamin, a protein bar
Htp 5, kava kava, St. Johns Wort, decaffeinated green tea, oatmeal
and two aspirin.

Looks like mornings here.

**Two Thoughts**

Don't mistake me for strong,

            I'm just numb; I hate it.

I'm damaged but not enough to just break,

            Like an old car that just won't die

I'm torn, worn and weathered,

            I just keep starting.  I've tried to stop

and I've tried to be optimistic

            but life just gets in the way.

## Please Open Your Eyes

I was speaking with a friend today with hopes of satisfaction
through acceptance of my new self,
my true self.

I found myself saddened when I found him battered by the same
things that I left,
to be me.

I asked myself, when I hung up the phone,
"How long does he have?"
What a waste, behind all the hope he is true.

## Heavenly Thoughts

I'm not waiting for heaven.
For that,
>                    some say I'll go to hell.

That doesn't sound so forgiving.
But I figure,
>                    every man for himself.

**I Saw a Crowd At Kerouac's Grave Today**

And thought,

You can dwell on the graves of dead poets in search of inspiration
and recreate uncertain poems of what might have been or you can
speak with your memories and find certain explanation in
everything you create.

and that's why I left college.

**1985**

I was five years old:

I remember how the sun was dry and hot.
I remember bee stings and ice cream at warm dusk,
fireflies, grasshoppers, backyard baseball and bike rides.
I remember getting the mail and scraped knees.
I even remember harmless boyhood fights and long car rides
but I don't remember feeling normal.

I remember all the questioning I'd do with myself.
I remember feeling insecure before I knew the term for it.
I remember knowing things but not knowing how or why I knew
        them.
I remember thinking, "When I am older I'll have it all figured out."

But I don't remember when I thought, "older" was.

**If I Had a Thought**

I'd throw it together on some piece of paper, dissect it into tiny little pieces, separate what is relevant to me and to others, compare the two and note the difference between the rest of the world and myself.

I do this with everything.

But right now, I don't have one.

Finally.

**Point Of View**

Of all the broken thoughts that other people use to build their idea

of who you are

there is never one that is completely true.

What truly matters is whether your thoughts are complete.

**Everything Becomes The Past**

In retrospect, it all seems to make sense.
Yet it is all so confusing in the moment.
I've found that since I've figured this out,

        so much worry is so very worthless.

## Mind Control

Close your mind out and let your heart lead,
let it guide your feet and you will see
that living life by what your mind has learned
can hold you back with useless concerns.

Forget your mind, it is fabricated
by everything your teachers gave it.
You've been taught to think like everyone else,
by your TV and radio, but not yourself.

Don't live your life in black and white,
your heart is not colorblind.
Don't make a living. Make a life.
Don't get married. Find a wife.

If you find you're lost, don't wait to be found,
make a map and you'll get out.
This is your life; it's long and hard,
don't make it harder; make it yours.

# IV. Autumn

------------ *I've found justice in Autumn*
*for all I've been through.* ------------

**Creativity**

All of this walking and talking and running and working,
this reaching and falling, the failing, succeeding;
it all will mean nothing unless there's something you're leaving.

It's no wonder we created a creator we can't see:
He's this life's only hope for those who are lazy.

There may be no meaning but there is always creativity.
This life will be nothing but what you've left for the world to see.

## Life Sense

I have spent a lot of time trying to make sense of life, searching for some sort of balance of all we endure and what we earn from it. I have been unsuccessful. The only conclusion I can seem to make is that life doesn't make sense. If life were sensible it would be just as one sided as it is now except on the complete opposite side of the scale. Wouldn't it be nice if it were always a good something being referred to whenever the expression, "It's always something." was used? Things would just seem so much more worth it if every time another person died we were left saying that they've had enough good in their life rather than the so much more common thought that, life is too short. I'm not sure which I should wish for more: All of this not to be true or that I'll somehow forget.

## Vision

Not with flawless vision or with an infinite amount of time could one stare long and hard enough to know another. There is no one with the ability to see the thoughts and memories I hold on to or those I work hard to forget. Not if I stood naked or allowed the focus of every living eye to be directed deep within my own could one see the world I know. Not even if I listed word for word upon my skin every fear, hope, regret, dream or vision that I have ever held could the reader find complete understanding of who I am. Sight cannot fully convey one's will, self-esteem, self-respect, faith, conflict, intention, belief, experience or even outlook. Yet it is still the only sense so many choose to use in so many situations.

## Chicken Or Egg

What is it really when someone hates you for what they did to you,
Bad luck?  On whose part?

I've had trouble understanding the way people allow selfishness to
completely deny them compassion.  I've been selfish at certain
points in my life but never enough to not feel bad about it.  Is that
the difference in people?  Like when you hear that saying about
how there are two types of people in this world and someone goes
on to list two traits, usually something like, "The quick and the
dead" or "The haves and the have nots."  Maybe that's just it,
maybe we are only made up two types of people:  The selfish and
the compassionate.  I'm not sure who said it but I once read a
quote that read, "Without pain there would be no compassion."
Maybe it's that, that divides us and it's all about those who've
been pained and those who cause pain.  That would help explain a
lot but it may wrap you up in a kind of chicken and egg type riddle.

## Stay On The Gray Road

There's a thin gray road that cuts through the cemetery, it's lined with stones that are marked with names and clever sayings that most times relate life to death. A lot of the time I'll read them and wish I had thought them up. Sometimes I wonder what my clever stone might read. I suppose I could write something, at least then it would be one less wish I missed out on. On the other hand, I'm not sure I'd want anything written on it at all. This thin gray road does a pretty good job relating life to death.

## Self Contradiction

I'm a mind wandering, analytical, obsessive,
living fairly simply.
I'm observant, soft-spoken and calmly received,
unlike my on-goings internally.
I've got a self-effacing way about me
that appears to be humility.
It's really just low self-esteem
and a lot of insecurity.
I've got an independent personality
which contradicts my past dependencies.
I'm sensitive and emotional
with severe depression tendencies.
I've sat face in hands, praying for death, bleeding life,
with my entire fate unknown.
I created strength out of all of it and
have somehow found some hope.
I live my life as a search for myself
and if that's selfish, I'm not sorry.
I'm loved by some and hated by others
for the truths I wish I didn't carry.
I have half of a mind learning from
all the defeat that I've endured
and half of a mind striving to defeat
the half I've learned.
I miss some things that I shouldn't
and I don't some things that I should.
I miss some people I shouldn't have to
and I've wished death on others to feel good.
Through pain, I've grown quite compassionate
which through ego, I'll sometimes hide.
I seemed to have kept the same self-perception

since about Nineteen Eighty Five.
I've got notebooks full of words
but most times I have no interest in speaking.
From time to time, I'll write something down
that may be worth someone reading.
Some of this is vanity,
but most of it's written to help me.
It isn't easy understanding yourself
when your life is this contradictory.

## Scar

Behind all of this scar, I am still a small boy, lost, sad and wonderful. I have immense amount of understanding of this and I miss not knowing sometimes.

When I fall into this zone of recollection and I'm stuck, sorting through my memory. It's a lot like looking into a shattered mirror; I become barely recognizable, incomplete, and end up with seven years of bad luck.

I'm cut by the pieces I've picked up and looked deep into and I know that I'll never get it all back together again but the blood on my hands reveals that this new mirror reflects a much clearer vision and that is where my focus will remain.

## Fistful Of Memories

I've looked deep into the shattered glass of the mirror that is my memory, sorted through my reflection all broken up and separated from itself; missing pieces, forgotten fragments and everything that is supposed to be whole but is now just sharp.

I've put back together some of these glass puzzles in my head, it seems all I end up with is deeper cut fingers; new openings to the scars I already knew were there. Scars that I mistakenly thought might disappear if I were to take a closer look.

From now on, I'll stay broken and work on holding together what's left of this reflection. I'm not big on hiding from yourself but I can learn to stop looking. Seeking satisfaction in being tiny pieces of glass, some sharp, some dull, some lost and some hidden is beginning to seem a more worthy task. No one else can see the mirror anyway. All they can see is me: The fist that was thrown into it.

**Hidden Windows**

It's hard not to notice what's really going on, once you've seen through.

Some people never even seem to notice the windows that are hanging behind all the decorative curtains that we string up daily, either that or they don't care.

I suppose we need that though, a little compensation for those of us who are stuck staring in awe at everything all around us.

Otherwise, things might begin to get better.

## Why Reality T.V. Scares Me

Day after day I am face to face with unearned authority and the far too often, speech before thought. I fear and wonder if it is human characteristic of us all to want to dictate others lives rather than leaving focus on our own. To me, it is a shame that so many of us decide to offer advice but not live it, to ignore any other point of view and pass judgment based solely on our own misguided truths or to simply and unknowingly allow our lives to pass us by as we become spectators and speculators of the lives around us.

As my own life seems to be growing into a routine and as I carry on doing the things that I do because they feel right for ME, I hope that I never lose hold of these fears and wonders. It is not often that I am complacent with being fearful or wondrous but this is what will continue to remind me to not fall into the hole of an idea that because it seems to work, it is the best, the only, or even scarier, that it is THE or that there is ANY, right way to live.

## My Overstuffed Jar

The jar will always be a jar no matter what it is filled with.
Usually the things that we fill them up with for some reason over-
    shadow and replace what it really is.

"Pass me the jelly."
"May I have the salt?"

It seems as though we do this with people as well.  Yet, it doesn't
matter how many things that I fill myself up with, whether in
search of definition or if it is gained by default, I, like the jar, still
possess the underlying naked truth and potential that connects me
to everybody else:  Emptiness.

## Vice Versa

Ninety-eight point six degrees, thin, a little sun burnt, in a padded
chair with a flooded memory.
I run through the list of thoughts that I work to ignore everyday.
It might not be a preferred way of life but it is what has kept me
from being:
Ice cold, swollen, pale white, motionless, underground and
thoughtless.
Or vice versa.

## I've Picked Enough Scabs

I've picked enough scabs and tasted enough of my own blood to realize that all this scratching at the surface will only leave me with a more prominent scar.  Whether I think I can force myself to forget certain things and move on is irrelevant to the fact that my mind will go wherever it decides to and in doing so I will acquire all the emotional souvenirs that is gained in all of its time travel.  I can sit and repeat to myself the typical slogans of, "Just let go" or "Let it be" but the fact that I have to sit and remind myself of such slogans shows that I haven't done very much of either.  I realize now more than ever that I will always carry with me all that I'm made up of, whether it is good or bad, wanted or unwanted and knowing there isn't much room for negotiation on my capacity for one or the other.  Believe me, knowing this doesn't take away the instinctual wanting to revert back to childish reactions of stomping my feet and whining, "This isn't fair."  Which I'll admit, does seem a much easier slogan to repeat and believe in.  But all in all, I think that a time does come, and that it may have just arrived, in which you stand up and realize that there's something much bigger happening; bigger than feelings, bigger than emotions and bigger than me and that it is time to just take some things for what they are.  Not because it's right, not because it's fair and certainly not because I feel redeemed but because the time has come when all that matters is no longer just me and with that comes the obligation to move my focus to what can be and away from what has already been done.

## 11 O'clock News

Everyone watches the news as is if it's not really happening all around their T.V. sets. They find compassion and even disgust at what they believe is going on whenever and wherever they aren't close by. But, so little of these same people take action all day long to make sure that eleven O'clock hour is a pleasurable one.

**October**

With pockets and fistfuls of emotion, I stand in front of years of trying times. Just in this past month alone, I've been a first hand witness to love, hate, birth and death; a summary of the collection of hours and minutes referred to as and for lack of a better term, my life.

I am completely coherent as to which portions of this ever spinning pie chart I prefer over the other but what scares me is the lack of control I have over its rotation.

I haven't always, but I now do my best to give my all in balancing this ball beneath my feet, at least in respect to my own life. Still, I can't help but feel uneasy about the fact that at anytime the ball could pop or be kicked out from underneath me by all, so much and any of which I have no control over. Yes, this does mean you and you and you and you and you and....

## Surety

At some point, I reached a point of surety. I'm not sure what brings it on exactly but there is now a definite difference in the want or need to defend my beliefs, opinions or lifestyle, when compared to that of past. Somehow, I've reached a point in which all of this seems unnecessary and I can't find it in myself to worry about whether or not someone agrees with or can understand my way of life or view of it. I think this is something that I have always somewhat wanted to attain without even knowing it. All the fighting may have been a reaction to the fact that I wasn't satisfied with just being and that I felt like others had to know why I was who I was but now I just do what I do because I do and because it feels right to me and that seems to be all that makes sense. I'm no longer faced with conflict or confusion, just simple, private living with no one to answer to. I have had to answer to people my whole life and now I am glad to have reached a point in which I will only answer to myself. Except now it seems the expectations are a bit higher.

## Day 10,372

I know a lot of people that love to say, "One day at a time" as an offering of hope or advice and I know a lot of people who count days since a day some time ago or until a day sometime in the future. I'm more the kind of guy who likes to take things as a whole and not splitting everything up into easily counted sections.

This is day ten thousand three hundred and seventy two.

When I see my life written out like that it really doesn't seem very long at all but when I think about all that has led up to now I don't get the same effect. It is amazing how much can be fit into such a short time. Much like when you have those dreams that seem like a full-length movie but somehow fit in between a 9 min snooze button interval.

I'll take the full-length movie over the nine-minute trailer any day.

This is probably due to my underlying desire to be seen for who I am as a whole and not itemized into the many interests, faults, talents, achievements and failures that I have acquired throughout the days of my life. However, I believe this desire is also a primary catalyst for why I have any interests, faults, talents, achievements and failures at all.

In some cases, the same traits that have gotten me in trouble have allowed me to attain my most cherished accomplishments.

**Comfort**

The goal is the same for all of us but how the goal is achieved is
what dictates our principles.

I wrote that the other day while arguing with myself into my
notebook about why some people find it so easy to ignore things
like honesty and loyalty and still seem to carry on appearing just as
comfortable as anyone else while others, as in my case, can be
accused of being, "Loyal to a fault" and "Brutally honest." Both
true characteristics of mine because of how uncomfortable I would
be in my own conscience if I were anything but.

For me, that is the goal: Comfort,

in my conscience, with my family, in my home, in my career, in
my life and when I die. Overall, I believe that we all just want to
be comfortable and that comfort is the goal that we are all
searching and fighting for. The difference in people isn't what
we're looking for,

the difference is whether we are willing to make others
uncomfortable getting there.

## Memories

What's buried is not forgotten
but it's buried all the same.
I don't dig up coffins
but I've been known to mourn at graves.
We can try to bury our memories
but they'll wake us when we sleep.
We can allow them to haunt us forever
or accept them and rest in peace.

## Autumn

After all the cemetery walks
and self-analytic talks,
the sulking and the wishing
for a less cold and uphill course,

I'm satisfied and self-aware
without a desire to explain my complacence.
I see no reason to defend the fruits
that I've acquired during infructescence.

I've shaken down trees
and left them bare,
I've watered new plants
to no avail.

Seasons change
and time has passed,
pain and loss
was all but lacked.

There are things that change
and things that don't,
things that will
and things that won't,

Truth can hurt
and truth can heal,
truth is in knowing
which truths to feel.

Forcing new seasons has
never changed much at all
but fall came without asking
and without my control.

Now, finally the cost
has been paid in full.
I've found justice in Autumn
for all I've been through.

www.DaveBreslin.com

ISBN 142518970-9